How to play

BASKET

G000088459

a step·by·step guide

Text:
Liz French

Technical consultants:
Mark Robinson and
Neil Mapletoft

JARROLD

Other titles in this series are:

AMERICAN FOOTBALL	**DINGHY SAILING**	**SQUASH**
BADMINTON	**GET FIT FOR SPORT**	**SWIMMING**
BOWLS	**GOLF**	**TABLE TENNIS**
COARSE FISHING	**HOCKEY**	**TENNIS**
CRICKET	**SNOOKER**	**WINDSURFING**
CROQUET	**SOCCER**	

How to play BASKETBALL
ISBN 0-7117-0487-2
First published in Great Britain, 1991
Text copyright © Liz French, 1991
This edition copyright © 1991 Jarrold Publishing
Illustrations by Malcolm Ryan

Designed and produced by
Parke Sutton Limited, Norwich
for Jarrold Publishing, Norwich

Contents

Introduction

Basketball began in America a hundred years ago and, although considered a 'new' game in the UK, has been an organised sport in England for over fifty years. Its fast-growing popularity in recent years is partly due to the famous Harlem Globetrotters whose dazzling displays of skill captured the imagination of millions of TV viewers. Its appeal is well-deserved, for few other games offer such a wonderful combination of individual skill and team effort.

Basketball is fast-moving, exciting and enjoyable both to play and to watch. Because there are only five players on each side, there are no restricted playing positions and every team member participates fully in the game at all times. You're certainly never left standing around while the action takes place at the other end of the court! The fact that every player needs to be able both to attack and defend only adds to the game's appeal. Because the terminology of the game can be confusing at first, unfamiliar words and phrases are printed in italics as they appear in the book and are defined in the glossary on page 48.

If you want to take up basketball for the first time, this book will help get you started. It will also be useful if you already have some experience of the game and want to improve your skills. The book offers all the basics — an outline of the game, step-by-step guidelines for developing techniques, hints on team and individual tactics and suggestions for practising. It is **not** intended to give comprehensive coverage of all the rules, but if you are serious about the game, you can obtain a copy of the official rule book from the English Basket Ball Association (EBBA) at Calomax House, Lupton Avenue, Leeds LS9 7EE.

If you've never played before, a good step is to join a club. This will give you access to coaching and, of course, the possibility of joining an established team playing against others (there are both local and national leagues in the UK). Ask at your local sports centre, or contact the EBBA, for details of clubs in your area: keen newcomers are always welcome. And as you'll see from this book, there's plenty you can do to develop and improve your passing, dribbling and shooting skills on your own in the meantime!

COURT AND EQUIPMENT

The Court

The standard indoor basketball court is 26m (85ft) long and 14m (46ft) wide. The playing surface is wood or any smooth, level artificial surface — its essential requirement is to allow the ball to bounce consistently. The whole area needs to be well lit and there should be a clearance of at least 7m (24ft) between the floor and ceiling. Chairs and other obstructions must be kept well clear — at least 2m (6ft) — of the boundary lines.

The aim of the game

The object of basketball is simple: to get the ball through your opponents' basket in order to score points — and to try to stop your opponents from doing the same.

The ball

The ball is made of rubber with an outer case of leather, rubber or a synthetic material. Weight and dimensions are as shown here, although they may vary slightly. The main requirement of the ball is that it bounces correctly — its rebound must be between 1.2m and 1.4m (4ft-4ft 8ins) when the ball is dropped from a height of 1.8m (6ft).

Circumference:
75-78cm
(29½-30¾ins)

Weight:
600-650gm
(20ozs-22ozs)

26m (85ft)

Restricted area (the *key*)
5.8m (19ft)

Free-throw line

Three-point line

6m (20ft)

Free throws
(see page 21)

0.85m (2ft 9ins)
0.85m (2ft 9ins)
0.3m (1ft)
0.85m (2ft 9ins)
1.75m (5ft 9ins)

1.25m (4ft)

Team be

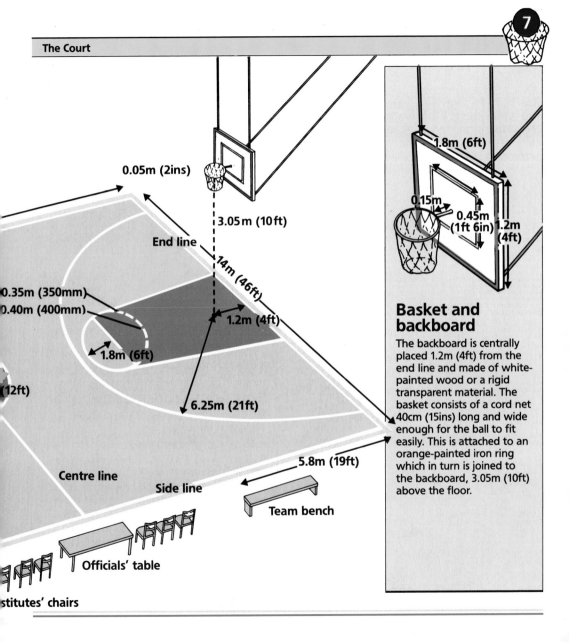

0.05m (2ins)

3.05 m (10 ft)

End line

14 m (46 ft)

0.35m (350mm)
0.40m (400mm)

1.2m (4ft)

1.8m (6ft)

(12ft)

6.25m (21ft)

Centre line

Side line

5.8m (19ft)

Team bench

Officials' table

stitutes' chairs

1.8m (6ft)

0.15m

0.45m (1ft 6in)

1.2m (4ft)

Basket and backboard

The backboard is centrally placed 1.2m (4ft) from the end line and made of white-painted wood or a rigid transparent material. The basket consists of a cord net 40cm (15ins) long and wide enough for the ball to fit easily. This is attached to an orange-painted iron ring which in turn is joined to the backboard, 3.05m (10ft) above the floor.

Dress

Shorts and a sleeveless vest are normally worn. The most important thing is that they are comfortable and don't restrict your movement. Members of a regular team wear identical kits, often provided by their club. Players are numbered between four and fifteen and their shirts display their number on front and back.

Footwear

You will be jumping and landing all through a game, so you need to take care of your feet and keep them comfortable! You can wear trainers but make sure they are well made and fit properly.

Hint box: choosing footwear

If you want to invest in some specialist basketball footwear:

- Go to a good sports shop.

- When trying a pair, lace them up properly and walk around to check fit.

- During a game you will probably find two pairs of socks best to protect against blisters — remember to make allowance for this.

- Look for a thick rubber sole for good grip.

- You can choose high-cut boots or low-cut shoes — this is a matter of personal preference, though many players find the high type give better ankle protection.

OFFICIALS AND PLAYERS

The Officials

The game is controlled by a referee and an umpire, helped by a scorer and a timekeeper. In top class games, there is also a 30-second operator.

Referee and umpire

Equipment:
A uniform of long grey trousers, grey shirt and basketball shoes.
A whistle!

Role:
- Jointly control the game, although the referee has ultimate control and the final decision on any point.
- Take up positions on opposite sides of the court — outside the boundaries as far as possible — and swap sides after each foul and before each *jump ball*.
- Keep a careful watch on the play and stop the game where necessary according to the rules.
- Use a number of hand signals to indicate their decisions, and a whistle to stop play.

Scorer

Equipment:
Official score sheet.
Five markers numbered 1-5.
Horn or bell to indicate when a substitute or *charged time out* is requested.

Role:
- Records the names and numbers of the players including substitutes (see page 11).
- Keeps a running check of all points scored.
- Indicates all fouls called against each player by raising the appropriate numbered markers.
- Keeps a record of all time-outs.

Timekeeper

Equipment:
A game stopwatch.
A time-out stopwatch.
A gong or bell (different from the scorer's) to indicate the end of playing time.

Role:
- Keeps a record of playing time and time of stoppages.
- Times the time-outs.
- Indicates the end of each half or overtime with the gong or bell.

Thirty-seconds operator
(see also page 14)

Equipment:
Thirty-second clock.

Role:
Operates the 30-second clock, starting it the moment a team takes possession of the ball.

The Players

Each of the two teams consists of up to ten players, but only five from each team are on court at any time during a match. Both teams will also have a coach who is responsible for deciding team tactics and substitutions.

One of the great things about basketball is that there are no positional restrictions — so all the players need to be versatile, able both to attack and defend. Players can, however, be divided into three main types:

Guards

These are usually the quicker members of a team and initiate attacking moves.
They tend to play furthest away from the basket.

Skills and attributes:
● Speed ● Long distance shooting ● Accurate passing

Forwards

These are normally taller than the guards and concentrate their play on either side of the *key.*

Skills and attributes:
● Shooting, especially from the edge of the key ● Passing — normally to centres ● Rebound play

Centres

Also known as *posts* or *pivots,* they are usually the tallest players in a team — or the best at jumping! They operate close to the basket.

Skills and attributes:
● Height ● Shooting from close in ● Rebound play ● Passing

Playing Positions

Teams can use different line-ups of players — and change the balance during a game depending on how the play develops and the strengths and weaknesses of the opposition. Here are two typical starting formations:

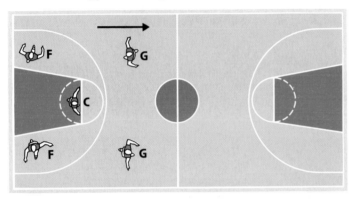

1. This is a 2-1-2 formation: two guards, one centre and two forwards. This is normally used as a defensive formation.

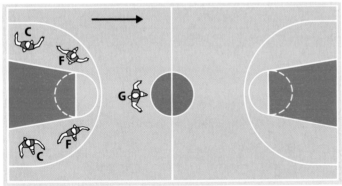

2. A 1-2-2 line-up: one guard, two centres and two forwards. Easiest to play and the most difficult for opponents to penetrate.

Substitutes

In such a fast-moving game, it would be impossible for the original five players of each team to keep up the pace and intensity throughout. So players are brought into and out of play according to the substitution rules.

● Any or all of the five players in action may be replaced by substitutes during a game.

● Substitutions can only be made when the ball is *dead* and the game clock stopped.

● Following a violation, only the 'innocent' team can make a substitution; but if they opt to do so, the other team can as well.

If the coach tells you to go on as a substitute you must:

● Report to the scorer.

● Sit on the bench until the scorer's signal is sounded.

● Stand up and indicate your intention to play to the nearest floor official.

● Wait to be beckoned by the official before entering the court.

The Game

The basic idea of the game is, of course, to score more points than your opponents. But to get the ball through your opponents' basket to score, your team must first get possession of the ball. Then you have 30 seconds (see page 14) to *dribble* or pass it to the net and shoot, all using hands only. The following pages will show you how a game is played and explain any potentially confusing rules.

Starting

The visiting team chooses ends for the first half (a coin is tossed if you're on neutral territory), and teams change ends at half-time. The game is started by a *jump ball* at the centre.

1. One player from each team stands in the centre circle on the halfway line, each on the side nearer to their own basket. The referee throws the ball up into the air between them. The other players must all stay outside the circle.

2. Both players try to tap the ball and get possession for their team — but the ball must not be touched until it has reached its greatest height.

3. A player involved in the *jump ball* may only touch the ball twice: after that it must be touched by one of the other players, or touch the basket, backboard or floor, before they can touch it again.

4. The *jump ball* procedure is also used at the beginning of the second half and periods of extra play, and to restart the game in certain situations (see page 15).

Duration

The game is divided into two 20-minute halves, with an interval (usually ten minutes) at the end of the first half. However, a full game usually takes about 90 minutes including stoppages and half-time.

Hint box: taking the jump ball

It's best to let your tallest player — or highest jumper — take the *jump ball*.

What if . . . the ball hits the floor before either player has touched it?
The *jump ball* is taken again.

Scoring

Teams score points for throwing the ball successfully through their opponents' basket. The number of points awarded depends on the type of shot and where it was taken from.

1

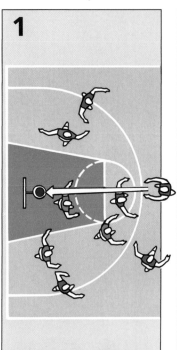

A *field goal* taken from outside the three-point line.
Three points.

2

A field goal taken from inside the three-point line.
Two points.

3

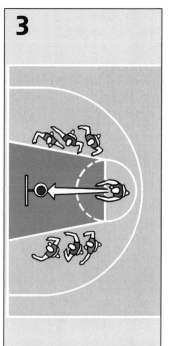

Scoring from a *free throw* (see page 21).
One point.

What if . . . there's a draw?

A game cannot end in a tie. If the scores are level at the full-time whistle, an extra five-minute period is played. As many extra periods as it takes to break the tie are played.

Time Limits

One of the reasons basketball is so exciting and fast-moving is that time limits are set for various actions. If you go over the allowed limits, your team loses possession and forfeits the ball to the other team.

Thirty seconds rule

As soon as your team gets the ball, the 30-second clock is started. You then have 30 seconds to try for a goal.

Ten seconds rule

If your team gets possession in your own half, you have ten seconds to advance it over the centre line.

Five seconds rule

On a *throw-in* or *free throw*, you have five seconds to put the ball in play. The same limit applies to any closely guarded player who has the ball — you must shoot, pass, roll or dribble the ball before the five seconds are up or the other team takes possession.

Three seconds rule

No member of the team in possession of the ball can stay in the opponents' restricted area (*key*) for longer than three seconds — though this does not apply while the ball is in the air on a try for basket, or during a rebound from the backboard, or if the player is attempting to leave the key.

Charged time-outs

Coaches can request two time-outs in each half of the game, and one in each five minute extra time period. These last one minute and give the coach a chance to discuss tactics. The intention must be relayed from the coach to the scorer, who in turn indicates to the official (referee or umpire). Play continues until the ball becomes *dead.* The clock is then stopped and the *charged time-out* begins and is carefully timed.

Stopping and Restarting

The game watch and time-out watch, as well as the 30-second clock (see opposite) are much-used and vital pieces of equipment during a game of basketball!

At the beginning of the game the game watch is started the moment the ball reaches its highest point. During the game, it is stopped at the end of each half or extra period and when the official blows the whistle for any of the following:

Cause	Restart procedure
1. A violation or foul.	Varies — see pages 19-21.
2. A held ball. Two or more players of opposing teams have one or both hands firmly on the ball or the ball is lodged in the basket supports.	Jump ball from nearest circle.
3. Ball goes out of bounds (over boundary lines).	Throw in. Official gives the ball to a member of the team not responsible for putting the ball out; this player stands out of bounds on the sideline near where the ball went out, and has five seconds to throw, bounce or roll it to another player. If the officials are in doubt as to who last touched the ball, a *jump ball* is taken.
4. Suspension of play for injury, *charged time-outs* or any other reason decided by officials.	Throw in by team in possession at time of stoppage, at nearest point on sideline. Time limit of five seconds.
5. 30-second signal is sounded. A team has gone over the time limit for possession of the ball.	Throw in by non-offending team at point on sideline nearest where ball was when signal sounded. Time limit of five seconds.

Note: After a basket
The clock does not stop after a basket is scored. An opponent of the scoring team throws the ball into court from behind the endline where the goal was scored. This must be done within five seconds of holding the ball.

Moving the Ball

Remember it's hands only.

● **You can use one or both hands to catch, control, pass or shoot.**

● **One hand only for dribbling.**   ● **You must not hit the ball with clenched fist.**

● **Deliberately playing the ball with your foot is a violation, though if you touch it accidentally with your foot you will not be penalised.**

● **The team in possession must not pass the ball back onto their half of the court. This would be a** *back court violation.*

When you get possession of the ball, you have three choices: dribble, pass or shoot.

Dribbling

You are entitled to dribble the ball whenever you get possession.

1

You must bounce the ball on the floor using one hand only. Once you've touched the ball, it must always bounce before you touch it again.

2

The dribble ends when you touch the ball with both hands at once, or let it rest on one or both hands. When the dribble ends, you must not begin another dribble until you have taken a shot, or the ball is played by another player.

If you opt to pass or shoot, the amount you are allowed to move depends on whether you are standing still or moving when you get the ball.

Getting possession when you are standing still . . .

If you are standing still when you get the ball from another player, or from a rebounded shot at the basket, you are not allowed to move with the ball. You can, however, *pivot*. This means one of your feet stays on the ground while you turn with the other. Once you are committed to pivoting on one or other of your feet, you cannot change your mind.

Pivot

. . . and on the move

If you collect the ball while on the move, you are allowed two steps **only** before shooting, passing or dribbling the ball. These two steps are executed in a particular way, called the *two-count rhythm*.

First count
● If one of your feet is already on the ground, the first count occurs just as you receive the ball.

● If both feet are off the ground when you receive it, the first count occurs when either or both of your feet touch the ground.

Second count
● The second count occurs when, after the count of one, you step onto the floor with one foot, or both feet touch the floor simultaneously.

This sounds much more complicated than it really is! In fact, when you receive a pass on the move, or when you're ending a dribble, you'll use either a stride stop or a jump stop.

Stride stop

Catch the ball with both feet off the ground, land on one foot and step forward on the other.

Jump stop

Catch the ball in the air and stop, landing on both feet simultaneously.
Once you have come to a legal stop, you may then pivot, but only on your **back** foot (the one-count foot). If your feet are together, you can use either.

Fouls

Although basketball is termed a no-contact sport, and all players must avoid contact with opponents, incidents between players do occur, sometimes accidental and sometimes deliberate. These are penalised in a variety of ways, with particular protection given to players in the act of shooting. Fouls can be either 'technical' or 'personal'.

When a foul occurs

- The referee blows the whistle and indicates his judgment on the severity of the foul (see below).

- The ball becomes dead.

- The offending player must raise an arm and turn to face the scorer.

- The scorer records the foul against the player.

- A player who has committed five fouls, personal or technical, must leave the court for the rest of the game.

- If a team has committed seven player fouls in a half, all further fouls committed when their opponents have the ball are penalised more heavily (see 'one-and-one rule', opposite).

What kind of foul?

1. Technical Foul	**Definition:** a foul against the spirit of the game, eg unsporting behaviour or language. **Penalty:** the other side is awarded two *free throws* or the option of a throw-in from the mid-point side line.
2. A Personal Foul	**Definition:** pushing, blocking, charging, illegal use of hands or any other contact. **Penalty:** varies according to severity of offence — see below.
a) Normal personal foul	**Definition:** for accidentally making contact with an opponent. **Penalty:** a throw-in from the side line nearest to where the foul occurred.
b) Intentional foul	**Definition:** deliberately causing contact with an opponent. **Penalty:** two *free throws* awarded to the other side (see f).
c) Disqualifying foul	**Definition:** unsporting behaviour, eg punching an opponent. **Penalty:** the offender is disqualified and a substitute brought on.
d) Double foul	**Definition:** when two players from opposing sides commit personal fouls against each other. **Penalty:** no penalty. A *jump ball* is taken.
e) Multiple foul	**Definition:** when two or more team-mates commit a personal foul on one opponent. **Penalty:** the other side is awarded two *free throws* (see f).
f) Foul on a player in the act of shooting	**Penalty:** if the goal is made it will count and a *free throw* is awarded. If it misses, two or three *free throws* are given.

One-and-one rule

After seven player fouls — either technical or personal — have been called against a team in one half, the one-and-one rule is brought into force. The player fouled is given one free throw. If a basket is scored from this, a second free throw is taken. If the first free throw is not successful, however, play continues.

At the end of the half, the seven team fouls are cancelled and the foul count starts again for the second half, though the fouls remain against the individual players.

Note: this rule only applies to fouls committed when the other team has the ball — if the offending team itself has possession when the foul is called, the penalty is as usual.

Personal fouls: whose fault?

The officials have to decide who is primarily responsible for any illegal contact, but you need to be aware of your responsibilities as a player in avoiding fouls.

1

You are entitled to occupy any part of the court not occupied by an opponent, provided you don't cause any personal contact in getting there.

Your 'personal space' occupies not just the floor but an imaginary vertical cylinder around your body.

2

If another player reaches into this imaginary cylinder and makes contact, it is her responsibility. Personal foul.

3

You may stick out a leg or arm, but not if this stops an opponent from moving past. Personal foul.

4

Just because you are trying to play the ball, this does not allow you to make contact with the player in possession. Personal foul.

5

When you are dribbling, you must expect players to move into your path. Until you get your head and shoulders past the opponent, it is your responsibility to get out of the opponent's way. Here the dribbler has not avoided the defender and is at fault. Personal foul.

6

When defending against a moving player who does not have the ball, you must give him time and distance to stop or change direction. Here defending player has blocked attacker. Personal foul.

7

You must not touch an opponent with your hand. If, however, you are trying to get the ball from an opponent and your hand incidentally makes contact with her hand while it is on the ball, this will not count as a foul — unless it's while she's trying to shoot.

8

Any flagrant unsporting foul — hitting or punching, for example — will get you disqualified. Disqualifying personal foul.

Free Throws

A free throw for a personal foul is awarded to the player who was fouled.

1 The thrower stands just behind (not on) the free throw line, 4.6 m (15 ft) from the basket.

2 The other players line up along the sides of the lane in the spaces marked out. The spaces nearest the basket are taken by two of the defending players, and the other players take alternate positions.

3 Once the official has given the ball to the thrower, the shot must be taken within five seconds. Opponents are not allowed to interfere.

4 Neither the thrower nor any other player may touch the line or the floor of the free-throw lane until the ball has touched the ring — or until it becomes obvious that it won't touch it.

Passing

Basketball is a team passing game. When you've got the ball, it may be more exciting to dribble and shoot, but if a team-mate is in a more advantageous position, an accurate pass gets the ball down court more quickly and safely. So don't neglect passing practice in your training sessions.

Chest pass

This is the most basic pass, used when there's no opponent between you and the receiver. It is used for quick, clean passing over short distances.

1 Hold the ball to your chest between the fingertips of both hands, elbows extended. For maximum power, your palms should not touch the ball.

2 Start the pass by extending your arms. Move your whole body in the direction of the pass.

3 At full stretch, snap your wrists forward and quickly release the ball. As you follow through, your fingers point at the receiver, and your thumbs down at the floor.

Hint box: passing

● Keep your eyes on your target.

● Make your passes low and direct so the ball is in the air for as short a time as possible to minimise the chances of interception.

● If your team-mate is moving, remember to time your pass so that it gets to where he's going, not where he's been!

● Try to disguise your intentions.

● Receivers should signal by extending a hand in the direction they want the ball to come — the side away from any defender. Aim your pass accurately to that point.

● As soon as you have passed the ball, move to a position where you can take a return pass.

Overhead pass

Used for passing over an opponent's head and especially useful for a taller player to use when passing over a smaller opponent. Remember to watch for, and aim at, your receiver's signal. A *javelin* pass also goes overhead and is designed for distance, speed and initiating fast breaks.

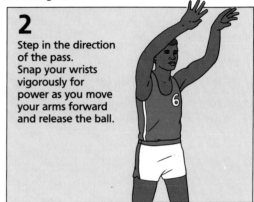

1
Start with the ball in both hands as for a chest pass, but held directly over your head. Note that the ball stays in front of your head.

2
Step in the direction of the pass. Snap your wrists vigorously for power as you move your arms forward and release the ball.

Bounce pass

Another way of passing when there is an opponent between you and your team-mate. Use with caution — this is a much slower pass and easier to intercept. It is most useful if your team-mate is not far away. You can make the pass with one or both hands — one is more usual.

1
Hold the ball in both hands and move in the direction of the pass.

2
Then take the ball to your side, by the hip, and push it away to bounce past the defender to your team-mate.

Getting Free and Catching

There is no point in making good passes if the receiver can't be relied on to catch the ball every time — and before you can receive a pass you must, of course, get free of your nearest opponent for an instant.

1 Step towards the defender who will be between your back and the basket.

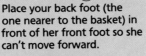

2 Place your back foot (the one nearer to the basket) in front of her front foot so she can't move forward.

3 Indicate to the passer where you want the ball by extending a hand.

4 Keep your eyes on the ball all the time. Once the pass has been made, take the ball in both hands with your fingers spread around it. Remember that your palms should not touch the ball.

5 Get the ball under control in both hands quickly and look to see what your next move is — dribbling, passing or shooting.

Hint box: catching

● **DO** keep watching the ball all the time.
● **DO** concentrate on making yourself an easy target for the passer — and make it clear where you want the ball to come.
● **DON'T** waste time once you have the ball.
● **DON'T** bounce the ball as you catch it — this will count as a dribble and prevent you from dribbling again this time.

Protecting the Ball

When you get possession of the ball, your opponents will immediately try to steal it away — so you must get into a position which protects the ball and disguises your intentions.

Wrong — ball held out in front.
This makes it easy for your opponent to steal the ball.

Wrong — ball held above head.
Here too the ball is very vulnerable.

Wrong — straight legs.
This wastes time — you'll have to bend your legs again to move off.

Right — ball held under chin, elbows spread, knees bent. Now your opponents have a much harder job to knock the ball away from you, and your bent knees mean you are ready to spring forward.

From this position — known as the triple threat position — you can either:

- Pivot (see page 17) to face the basket you're attacking.

- Take the ball up to shoot.

- Pass the ball to a team-mate.

- Start a dribble.

Dribbling

Dribbling — bouncing the ball with one hand — is another way of moving the ball around the court and is a skill you should practise hard to perfect. As a beginner, practise the action from a stationary position until you have the basic technique, then start moving around.

Practise until you can:

- Dribble without looking at the ball.   ● Dribble equally well with both hands.
- Change speed and direction quickly and easily to dodge opponents.

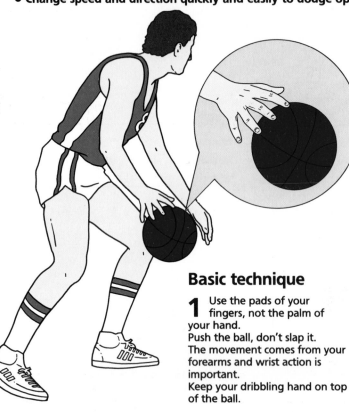

2 Make sure only one hand touches the ball — if both come into contact with it at once, the dribble will be deemed over.
If you're using your right hand, bounce the ball on the ground slightly in front of you and to the side of your right foot.

3 For the left-hand dribble, bounce it slightly ahead and to the side of your left foot.

4 Don't bounce the ball too high — keep it between knee and waist height.
Don't bounce the ball too far in front of you — opponents will easily steal the ball if you do.
Do try not to look down at the ball — you need to be able to see what your team-mates and opponents are doing.

Basic technique

1 Use the pads of your fingers, not the palm of your hand.
Push the ball, don't slap it.
The movement comes from your forearms and wrist action is important.
Keep your dribbling hand on top of the ball.

Once you have mastered the basic technique, you will need to practise dribbling in different situations.

Protected dribble

Your opponents will, of course, be doing all they can to get the ball away from you, so learn how to protect the ball from a close defender.

1 Bounce the ball close to your foot on the side away from the defender. Always keep your body between the ball and the defender. Keep your knees bent and your head up.

2 Let the shoulder nearest your opponent drop and bar the way with your arm.

Speed dribble

To break away from a defender, you will sometimes need to dribble at top speed.

1

You can speed up by pushing the ball further ahead when you are running into unmarked space . . . but remember to keep your head up.

2

Gather the ball safely at the end of the bounce and be ready to revert to a protected dribble as soon as a defender closes in.

Changing hands

To keep the ball away from defenders, you will often have to change hands.
There are several ways you can do this.
Remember that you must only touch the ball with one hand at a time.

Cross over

Change the ball from one hand to the other
by letting it bounce in front of you. Keep the
bounce fast and low so it is out of your hand
for as short a time as possible.

Between the legs

This is an advanced technique needing plenty
of practice, but gives good protection to the
ball and looks very impressive! Here the player
passes the ball from her right to left hand. She
has her left leg forward as she bounces the
ball between the legs . . . and collects it in her
left hand.

3

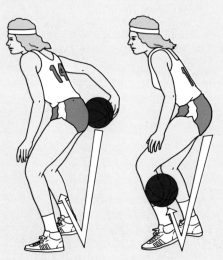

4

Behind the back
Another flashy-looking and very useful technique, but you'll need lots of practice to master it. Twist your fingers on the ball as it passes behind you to send it bouncing towards the other hand.

Reverse
For this slightly easier method you actually turn right round as you change hands. You have to be very quick and alert to danger as you will momentarily be facing away from the basket.

Here the player changes from a left-handed to right-handed dribble. The right foot is placed ahead and he pivots backwards on it a full 360°, bouncing the ball with his left hand. His right hand comes round to collect the ball.

Shooting

Shooting is probably the most exciting and enjoyable part of the game. It is also, of course, vital for scoring! There are several different types of shot to practise.

Lay-up shot

This is one of the most often-used shots, taken on the run from the left or right side of the basket. This sequence shows a shot made with the right hand to the right of the basket. The take-off jump is from the left foot. The procedure is reversed for a left-hand shot.

1 At the end of the dribble, or after receiving a pass, remember you are allowed just two steps. The first step here is on the right foot. The ball is safely in both hands and you should look up to see where you are going to shoot.

2 Your second step is the take-off step — here on the left foot. This is a longer step, building up momentum.

3 As you jump, take the ball up with both hands.

4 Then, at full stretch, release the ball with the hand opposite your take-off foot (here the right hand). Aim to hit the backboard gently at the top right-hand corner of the marked square.

Set shot

This is useful for shooting from a distance and when there is an opponent between you and the basket. Your stance is very important here, so practise regularly until you have it exactly right.

1 Your feet should be comfortably apart and pointing in the direction of the shot, with shoulders square to the basket. Bend your knees slightly to give yourself more power.

2 You can shoot with either hand. The ball rests on the finger pads — **not the palm** — of your shooting hand; the other hand is just used for support at the side. Note how the bent-back wrist makes a 'platform' for the ball.

Keep your eyes on the target.

3 Straighten your legs and release the ball just above your head, with a snapping wrist action and good follow-through. Think of 'waving goodbye to the ball'.

Hint box: taking free throws
(see page 21)

There is really no excuse for missing a free throw, and there are only three points to remember:

● Use the set shot technique.
● Keep calm and concentrate.
● **Practise** at every possible opportunity.

Jump shot

Once you have mastered the set shot technique you can progress to using a jump shot, which gives better protection from blocking. The technique is the same, but this time you release the ball at the top of a vertical jump.

1

Preparing for a jump shot — the stance is as for a set shot. Note the elbow of the shooting arm is right underneath the ball, with the upper arm at right angles to the forearm and at shoulder height.

2

Keeping your eyes on the target, straighten your legs and jump straight up — be careful not to go forwards or sideways.

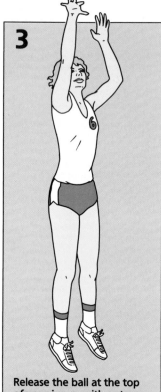

3

Release the ball at the top of your jump, with a strong flick of the wrist and full follow-through.

Close-up shots

When you are close to the basket your opponents will be marking you very closely. Here are some techniques for shooting under pressure.

Dunk shot

This shot requires good timing and a jump that gets you high enough to push the ball **downwards** through the ring. You need to be very tall, or an exceptional jumper to dunk successfully . . . but if you can perfect the technique, it is extremely impressive and excellent for your team's morale. Practise jumping and see if you can get your hands over the height of the ring. You can dunk with one or both hands, forwards or backwards, and from a standing or running position.

A dunk is sometimes called a *stuff*.

Hook shot

This is a one-handed shot made from close up and to one side of the basket. Similar to a lay-up, it is a softer shot than a dunk and often carried out by the *post* player facing away from the basket.

1. Here the shooter has received the ball on the left side of the key with his back to the basket. He immediately pivots to face the basket and steps sideways with his left foot, watching the target all the time.

2. As he jumps off his left leg, the ball is taken up in both hands, then released with the right arm fully extended. The wrist flicks through to give the ball backspin so it hits the ring gently.

Rebound Play

Even top teams only score with around 55 per cent of their shots, and when the ball rebounds off the back board it's up for grabs.
Rebound play is therefore a vital skill for both defending and attacking players.

Attacking

Basketball is all about teamwork. You need to practise working together not only to set up shots but to get team-mates into position to pick up rebounds. The forwards and centre are usually the rebound specialists.

1 Try to grab the rebound with both hands to protect the ball, and jump up to attempt another basket immediately.

2 If you can't get hold of the ball with both hands, try to tip it back through the ring with your fingertips. Even if it doesn't go through, it may give a team-mate another chance to keep the ball alive.

Hint box: attacking rebound play

Use your knowledge of your team-mates' style of shooting.

● **If someone tends to shoot short of the basket, their shots are more likely to bounce away from the front of the ring.**

● **If a player usually shoots long, the ball will rebound off the side or back of the ring.**
As the shot is made anticipate where it will rebound if it misses the basket and move into position to deal with this.

Defending

Every time your opponents miss a shot, you have a chance to gain possession of the ball and start an attack. To do this, all five attackers will need to be *blocked out* by your team so that they can't get to the ball. You don't have to be tall to block out successfully.

1

Make sure you stay between the player you are blocking and the basket. As the shot is made, step towards her.

2

Immediately pivot so your back is turned towards her, spreading your legs and elbows, knees bent so you are almost sitting on her lap. This makes it difficult for her to jump. Keep your eye on the basket, and go with her if you feel her move.

3

You then have a better chance of getting to the rebound — even if you're smaller than your opponent.

Hint box: defending rebound play

● A tall attacker's height is less of an advantage the further he is from the basket — so try to keep him well away from it.

● Once the rebound is taken you must move the ball out of the *key* area quickly — make a wide *outlet pass* immediately to a player near one of the sidelines.

● Many baskets are scored after rebounds by playing a *fast break* — moving the ball very quickly down the court before the other team has time to rally its defence.

Individual Defence

When your team doesn't have the ball, your job is to make life as difficult as possible for the attacking team so that you either steal the ball or force them to run out of time or make a bad shot. There are various tactics you can employ as a team (see pages 40-43), but here are some hints for individual defence.

Your over-riding aim in defence is to stop the attacking team from scoring!
This means . . .

● Keeping attackers away from the 'danger area' — the *key* you are defending.
Keep up the pressure until they have to pass the ball away from the basket.

● Making it hard or impossible for an attacker to shoot from an advantageous position close to the basket.

● Making it difficult for the attacker to run past you to collect a rebound or receive a pass.

● Forcing mistakes — a bad pass, a missed shot.

Hint box: individual defence

● **KEEP UP the pressure.**

● **WATCH your opponents to identify their strengths and weaknesses, then**

● **EXPLOIT that knowledge (can someone only dribble with their right hand . . .? Is that player weak on overhead passes . . .?).**

● **ANTICIPATE what the opposition is trying to do.**

● **STAY between your opponent and the basket.**

● **BE READY AND ALERT to help a team-mate or to start attacking when your team gets possession.**

Basic defensive positions

The basic stance for defending against an opponent who has the ball is important — practise with team-mates.

- Use your hands and arms as well as your body to challenge your opponent's attempts — but be careful not to make contact or you will be penalised.

- Knees should be slightly bent, feet flat on the floor and shoulder-width apart, with one foot ahead of the other. This gives you the flexibility to move or jump quickly with your opponent.

- Watch your opponent's stomach, not the ball. You are less likely to be fooled by a *fake*.

How far away you position yourself from your opponent is important too.

1 Wrong. Too close. The player will easily dribble past you.

2 Wrong. Too far away. The player will be able to shoot.

3 Right. To defend effectively you need to be about an arm's length from your opponent.

Defending close to the basket

Defending out of shooting range

This is obviously where effective defending is most critical, because everything happens so fast and any mistake is likely to result in a score for your opponents.

Keep one arm up to discourage a shot; the other should stay low in case of a dribble attempt.

Be ready to jump to defend if your opponent does shoot — but be careful not to be taken in by a fake, or you could be in the air at the wrong time!

Here the basic stance is the same, but keep your hands stretched out at your sides, palms up ready to get at the ball.

If the player is dribbling, keep one hand low by the ball — be careful not to touch the player or you will be penalised.

Get your hands up if she attempts a pass.

Moving with your opponent

When defending, you must stay alert and be ready to react to any move the attacker makes, sliding or shuffling forwards, backwards or sideways whilst maintaining your basic defensive stance.

1

As the attacker moves to his right in a dribble, the defender pushes his left foot out to the side, then slides the right foot over to meet it.

2

Here the attacker moves forward towards the defender who pivots by dropping one foot back (called a 'drop step') and sliding backwards at an angle. This way his upper body is still facing the attacker.

3

This time the attacker has moved backwards and the defender has to shuffle forwards. Note the hand held up to hinder a shot or pass.

Hint box: moving in defence

● Shuffle with small steps: don't bring your feet together or cross them over.

● Keep your knees bent and back straight.

● Never turn sideways on to your opponent — this makes you much easier to get past.

● Always try to force the attacker away from the basket.

● Keep up the pressure.

Team Defence

The previous pages outlined the individual skills needed when defending — but never forget that basketball is a team game. You must always know what your team-mates are doing, and work together to stop your opponents scoring and regain the ball for your own team. Teams use two main kinds of defence — *man-to-man* and *zone* — and you need to be able to play both.

Man-to-man defence

This is as it sounds, with one player marking one opponent. The nearer the play is to the basket, the closer you must mark.

Make sure you are always between your opponent, the ball and your basket.

Think of yourself as one point of a triangle, with the basket and the player with the ball forming the other two points.

As soon as the player you are marking gets the ball, hassle him. Don't let up the pressure: force him into rushing his actions and making a mistake.

Be ready to help a team-mate if the attacker gets through.

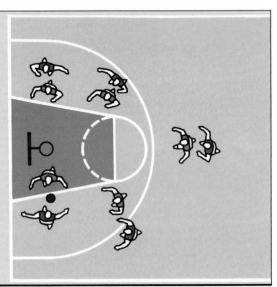

Hint box: man-to-man defence

Match up your players:

- A 6ft 4 ins (1.9m) player against a 5ft 7ins (1.7m) is not good.
- An 18 stone (114kgs) player against a 12 stone (76kgs) player is not good.
- A bad defender against a star ball player is not good.
- Be aware of substitutions and how they will affect your man-to-man tactics.

Man-to-man variations

1. Sagging man-to-man

Here you pick up your opponent as soon as he crosses the halfway line.
Sometimes known as a *half court press*.

2. Pressing man-to-man

With this defence, sometimes known as a *full court press*, you pick up your opponent as soon as your team loses possession or, more commonly, after a basket is scored. This is a very energy-consuming tactic and not used for long periods.

Attacking section   Defending section

Zone defence

Instead of marking one player, here you are responsible for a section of the court, picking up any attackers who come into your zone. The idea is to protect the *key* so that attackers cannot get in: so any shots taken will have to be from outside the key, with less chance of success. There are several different zone defences: this diagram shows a typical 2-1-2 formation — the two smaller players (guards, A & B) at the front of the key, the tallest player (C) in the middle and the two forwards (D & E) at the back of the key.

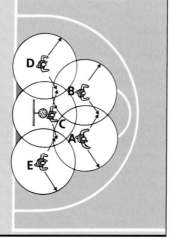

Hint box: zone defence

● If you are closest to the ball-carrier, make sure he cannot make an accurate pass into the *key*.

● Keep your hands up to stop attackers getting into the *key*.

● If a shot is tried, watch for the rebound — don't let them get it!

● Keep in touch with your team-mates — tell each other where your opponents are going.

Team Offence

A team offence is an organised style of attack designed to get you working as a team, so you can:

● **Set up scoring opportunities.**   ● **Overcome the defence.**   ● **Get into position for rebounds.**

There are different attacking styles to use against different defence tactics.

Fast break

Probably the best all-round system of attack. A fast break starts the instant your team wins possession, especially after the opposition have scored. The aim is to get the ball into scoring range before your opponents have time to set up their defence. If the defence is outnumbered, you should be able to *lay-up* or shoot. The critical point of any fast break is the first pass.

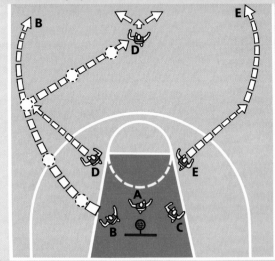

A typical fast break

A, B or C can take a rebound. In a typical situation, B takes the rebound.
D and E cut to the sideline.
B passes to D, and follows the ball.
D dribbles to the centre of the field.
B and E move ahead of the ball. D now has the option of passing to either.

Hint box: team attack

● Spread out — keep space between your team-mates.
● Get free ahead of the team-mate with the ball.   ● Look ahead — face the basket you are attacking.

Attack against man-to-man

1. Screen play

This is the most effective tactic to use against a basic *man-to-man* defence and should be included in your regular team practice as often as possible. The idea is to get the team member with the ball free to drive and score by putting a 'screen' between him and his defender. The 'screen' is another member of your team.

Players not involved in the screen must keep the basket area free so that the protected player can drive to score.

Attacker A dribbles, attacker B stands still, defender X defends by drop-stepping and bumps into B. A is then free.

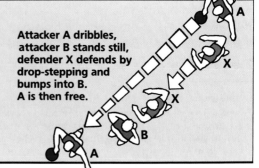

Attack against zone defence

1. Go for an outside shot

The greatest weakness of the *zone defence* is that it has no answer to a good outside shot. This is because the zones usually only cover the *key*. As the attacking team, you must exploit that weakness. Since the ball can be moved quicker than the defender can act, a good outside shooter can be given an uninterrupted shot. Even if this fails, it forces the zone to spread to meet the threat of your outside shooter, and this in itself weakens the defence and makes it easier to penetrate the key.

Attacker A passes ball to attacker B. Attacker B shoots from the outside of the zone. Attackers C and D move to draw the defenders.

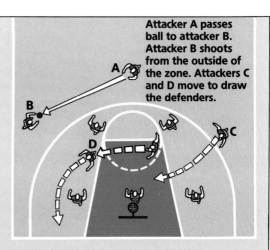

2. Overload

Another way of beating a zone defence is to overload one part or side of the zone by concentrating your players there. A combination of quick passing and superior numbers can often result in one free player and an uninterrupted shot.

Practice

If you are serious about improving your game, regular practice is vital — and a little every day is better than a long session once a week. As well as training with your team, you can

1 Dribbling

- Practise dribbling right-handed and left-handed to the halfway line and back.
- Use a 'through legs' or 'behind the back' hand change (see pages 28-29) as you get more proficient.
- Always keep your head up and look where you are going.
- Introduce cones and dribble around them making a figure of eight.

2 Lay-up shots

- Practise 25 from the right and 25 from the left.
- Shoot with the appropriate hand — get used to shooting with your weaker hand.

3 Hooks and jump shots

- Starting with the ball on one side of the key, drive under the basket to the far side and go for a hook.
- Collect the ball, dribble to the edge of the key and try a jump shot.
- Repeat 25 times on each side.

practise dribbling and shooting on your own. Here are some additional skills and drills to help you develop a good 'feel' for the ball. They are fun to do and should become a regular part of your practice sessions.

4 Shooting stations

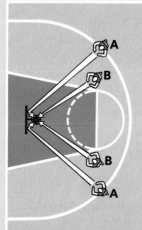

Identify two spots on either side of the key as shown: A one step away, B two steps away.

● A aims to get the ball into the basket off the backboard (a *bank* shot).
● B sends the ball straight through the ring (a *swish* shot).

5 Passing

● Stand 15ft (4.5m) away from a wall and practise passing against it.
● Aim at a particular spot on the wall.
● Practise chest, bounce and overhead passes.
● Move further back as you improve.

6 Rebounding (jump-catch-shoot)

● Stand 6ft (1.8m) straight back from the basket.
● Jump and shoot at the backboard, then jump, catch and shoot at the backboard again.
● Repeat without letting the ball touch the ground between shots.
● Make sure you are always in the air as you catch and shoot.
● When you can do nine consecutively, shoot the tenth for the basket.
● Practise on both sides on the basket (i.e. to the left and right of the basket).

Warm-Up

Before a game or practice session it is essential to prepare your muscles and joints for what
is to follow. This means warming up your muscles gradually for a minimum of five minutes,
and preferably ten or fifteen. You can use any gentle stretching and loosening exercises, but
here are a few suggestions.

1 Whole-body warm-up

Skipping is particularly good
for basketball,
strengthening your legs and
helping your footwork.
Light running or using an
exercise bike are also good.
Minimum two minutes.

2 Arm circling

Swing your arms through
their full range of
movement, brushing your
ear with each swing. Do
four each arm, then four
together, then repeat.

3 Side bends

Stand with feet apart and
hands on hips. Bend at your
hips, first to the left, then to
the right. Keep your head at
right angles to your body.
Repeat ten times.

4 Hamstring stretch

Sit on the floor, legs
together and straight in
front of you. Place your
hands on your thighs, then
slowly stretch as far down
towards your ankles as you
can. Hold for six seconds,
then slowly return to the
upright position. Repeat
four times.

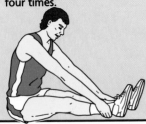

5 Groin and inner thigh stretch

Sit up with your legs as
wide apart as possible,
knees locked. Slowly reach
forward as far as you can to
a point on the ground
midway between your feet.
Hold for six seconds, then
return to the upright
position. Repeat six times.

6 Thigh stretch

Stand with support from a
wall or chair. Keeping your
back straight, bend
one knee to raise
your foot behind
you, grasping it
with your free
hand and
pulling it
up and
back.
Hold for six
seconds.
Do four for
each leg.

Fitness

Basketball is a fast and energetic game requiring speed, strength and stamina as well as suppleness. So try to include some general fitness training in each practice session. After your warm-up (see opposite) you may like to do any or all of the exercises on this page. For each, work for 20 seconds, rest for 20 seconds, then repeat or go on to the next exercise.

Speed

1. Speed skipping

Skip at maximum speed for 20 seconds, either on the spot or moving backwards, forwards or sideways.

2. Sprinting

Sprint from a standing start for a count of 20.

Strength

1. Press-ups

Do full press-ups if you can. If not, use this kneeling version. With your arms taking most of the weight, bend to lower your upper body to the floor, then raise yourself back up. Don't sag in the middle!

2. Squats

Stand with feet shoulder width apart, toes forward, and squat down until your hips are level with your knees. If you find you tip forward, raise your heels slightly with a book or other platform.

Stamina

1. Bench stepping

Step on and off a bench (or a bottom stair) as many times as you can in 20 seconds.

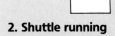

2. Shuttle running

When you can use the court, sprint back and forth between the end lines, bending to touch the line at each end. This is excellent for building your stamina.

Glossary

This glossary explains terms encountered in the text and some others you will hear when playing or watching the game.

ASSIST — A good pass which lets the receiver score easily.

BACK COURT — The half of the court a team is defending, i.e., containing its own basket.

BACK COURT VIOLATION — When the team in possession passes the ball back into its own half of the court.

BANK SHOT — A shot which bounces off the backboard into the basket.

BASEBALL PASS — A single-handed, overhead pass.

BASKET — The target, and the name for a score. A successful basket is worth one, two or three points.

BLOCK OUT/ BOX OUT — To block attacking players to prevent offensive rebound play.

BOX OUT — See *block out*.

CHARGED TIME-OUT — A stoppage of up to one minute, requested by a team's coach for instructing their players. Each team is allowed two time-outs per half, and one in each extra time period.

'D' — Used as an abbreviation for defence.

DEAD BALL — Ball not in play, owing to crossing the sidelines, or an infringement, or a basket being scored.

DOUBLE TEAM — Two defenders marking one attacker.

DRIBBLE — Move with the ball by bouncing it on the floor with one hand (see p16).

DUNK — Also known as a *stuff*, this is a spectacular *basket* scored when a player jumps up and thrusts the ball through the net from above.

FAKE — A pretence at moving the ball or your body one way whilst actually going another; designed to wrong-foot an opponent.

FAST BREAK — A quick move from a defensive position after gaining possession, designed to create a scoring chance before the opposition re-forms their defence.

FIELD GOAL — A *basket* scored from open play. Worth two or three points, depending on where it is scored from (see p13).

FREE THROW — An unopposed penalty throw awarded for a rule infringement and taken from the free throw line. Worth one point if a *basket* is scored.

FRONT COURT — The half of the court containing your opponents' goal.

FULL COURT PRESS — A man-to-man pressure defence tactic using the whole court, not just the defending team's half. Also called a *pressing man-to-man*.

HALF COURT PRESS — A man-to-man pressure defence tactic in the defending team's half of the court. Also called a *sagging man-to-man*.

HOOK SHOT — Single-handed shot from a side-on position to the basket.

JAVELIN — Another name for a *baseball pass*.

JUMP BALL — A method of starting or restarting play, where an official throws the ball up between two opposing players (see p12).

JUMP SHOT — Single-handed shot released at the top of a jump.

KEY — The key-hole shaped restricted area at the end of each court.

LAY-UP — Single-handed shot delivered at the end of a run, which hits the backboard before going into the basket.

MAN-TO-MAN — A defence system where each defending player marks a specific attacking player (cf *zone defence*).

OUT-OF-BOUNDS — A player is out-of-bounds if part of his/her foot is on, or over, a side-line or end-line.

OUTLET PASS — A quick pass by a defending player gaining possession after a rebound.

PIVOT — Rotate forwards or backwards on one foot. Also another name for a centre player.

POST — Another name for a centre player, usually the tallest player in a team.

PRESSING MAN-TO-MAN — See *full court press*.

SAGGING MAN-TO MAN — See *half court press*.

STRONG SIDE — The side of the court where the attacking team has possession of the ball.

STUFF — See *dunk*.

SWISH SHOT — A shot which goes straight into the basket without touching the backboard.

THREE-POINT BASKET — A score from outside the three-point (22 foot, 6.7m) arc.

THREE-POINT PLAY — When a player is fouled whilst scoring a field goal and gains another point from the *free throw*.

TRAVELLING — An illegal *dribble* in which the player fails to bounce the ball correctly.

TWO-COUNT RHYTHM — The two steps allowed after collecting the ball on the move (see p17).

THROW IN — Procedure for restarting play in certain circumstances (see p15).

WEAK SIDE — The side of the court where the attacking team does not have possession of the ball.

ZONE DEFENCE — A defence system where each defending player covers a specific area of the court (cf *man-to-man*).

Printed in Italy